EMMANUEL JOSEPH

Threads of the Earth, How Fashion, Ecology, and Ethics Weave a Sustainable Future

Copyright © 2025 by Emmanuel Joseph

All rights reserved. No part of this publication may be reproduced, stored or transmitted in any form or by any means, electronic, mechanical, photocopying, recording, scanning, or otherwise without written permission from the publisher. It is illegal to copy this book, post it to a website, or distribute it by any other means without permission.

First edition

This book was professionally typeset on Reedsy.
Find out more at reedsy.com

Contents

1	Chapter 1: The Fabric of Our Lives	1
2	Chapter 2: The Roots of Sustainable Fashion	3
3	Chapter 3: The Environmental Impact of Fashion	5
4	Chapter 4: Ethical Fashion and Fair Trade	7
5	Chapter 5: Innovations in Sustainable Materials	9
6	Chapter 6: The Role of Technology in Sustainable Fashion	11
7	Chapter 7: The Role of Fashion Designers in Sustainability	13
8	Chapter 8: Consumer Empowerment and Conscious Consumption	15
9	Chapter 9: The Intersection of Fashion and Climate Change	17
10	Chapter 10: The Cultural Significance of Sustainable Fashion	19
11	Chapter 11: Circular Economy and Fashion	21
12	Chapter 12: The Power of Policy and Regulation	23
13	Chapter 13: Community-Based Fashion Initiatives	25
14	Chapter 14: The Future of Fashion: Trends and Predictions	27
15	Chapter 15: Educational Initiatives and Sustainable Fashion	29
16	Chapter 16: The Intersection of Art and Sustainable Fashion	31

1

Chapter 1: The Fabric of Our Lives

In a world bustling with constant change, few things remain a steadfast companion like the clothes we wear. From the simple tunics of ancient times to today's cutting-edge fashion, our attire reflects our cultures, identities, and aspirations. The journey of a garment is a tale woven with threads of history, tradition, and innovation. It's not just about fabric and fashion; it's about how we express ourselves and interact with the world around us. In this chapter, we explore how fashion has evolved through the ages, the role it has played in society, and the impact it has on our daily lives.

As we delve deeper into the world of fashion, we uncover the intricate processes that bring a piece of clothing to life. It begins with the cultivation of natural fibers like cotton, flax, and wool, or the synthesis of artificial materials like polyester and nylon. These fibers are spun into yarns, which are then woven or knitted into fabrics. The journey from raw material to finished garment involves a symphony of skilled hands, advanced machinery, and innovative techniques. Each step is a testament to human ingenuity and craftsmanship, creating pieces that are not only functional but also works of art.

However, the fashion industry is not without its challenges. The pursuit of fast fashion, characterized by rapid production and low-cost garments, has led to a myriad of environmental and ethical concerns. The demand for ever-changing trends has resulted in overproduction, waste, and exploitation of labor. The fashion industry has become one of the largest polluters in the world, contributing to water pollution, greenhouse gas emissions, and landfill overflow. It's clear that the current system is unsustainable and calls for a reimagining of how we produce and consume fashion.

The shift towards sustainable fashion is gaining momentum, driven by a growing awareness of the industry's impact on the planet and people. Designers, brands, and consumers are increasingly embracing eco-friendly practices, from using organic materials and recycled fabrics to adopting fair trade and ethical labor practices. This movement is not just about reducing harm; it's about creating a new paradigm where fashion can be a force for good. By making conscious choices, we can weave a future where style and sustainability go hand in hand.

2

Chapter 2: The Roots of Sustainable Fashion

The roots of sustainable fashion can be traced back to ancient civilizations that lived in harmony with nature. Indigenous communities around the world have long practiced sustainable methods of textile production, using natural fibers and dyes, and adhering to principles of zero waste. These time-honored traditions offer valuable lessons for contemporary fashion, reminding us that sustainability is not a new concept but a return to our roots. In this chapter, we explore the wisdom of indigenous practices and how they can inspire modern sustainable fashion.

Traditional textiles like the Andean alpaca wool, Indian khadi, and African kente cloth are not only beautiful but also sustainable. These textiles are often handwoven, dyed with natural pigments, and crafted with care and respect for the environment. They embody the principles of slow fashion, where quality and longevity are prioritized over quantity and disposability. By reviving and celebrating these traditions, we can preserve cultural heritage while promoting sustainable practices.

The journey towards sustainable fashion is also fueled by innovative technologies and materials. Advances in biotechnology have led to the development of bio-based fabrics like mushroom leather, algae fibers, and lab-grown silk. These materials offer a sustainable alternative to traditional textiles, reducing the reliance on fossil fuels and minimizing environmental impact. Additionally, digital technologies like 3D printing and virtual prototyping are revolutionizing the design and production process, enabling more efficient use of resources and reducing waste.

Consumer awareness and activism play a crucial role in driving the sustainable fashion movement. As consumers become more informed about the impact of their choices, they are demanding transparency and accountability from brands. Grassroots initiatives, social media campaigns, and ethical fashion influencers are amplifying the message of sustainability and inspiring positive change. By supporting brands that align with their values and advocating for systemic change, consumers have the power to transform the fashion industry from the ground up.

3

Chapter 3: The Environmental Impact of Fashion

Fashion's impact on the environment is multifaceted and profound. The journey of a garment from raw material to retail store involves several stages, each contributing to pollution and resource depletion. The cultivation of natural fibers like cotton and the production of synthetic materials such as polyester have significant ecological footprints. Cotton farming, for instance, is water-intensive and often relies on pesticides and fertilizers, leading to soil degradation and water contamination. On the other hand, polyester production involves petroleum-based processes that emit greenhouse gases and contribute to climate change.

The dyeing and finishing processes are also environmentally taxing. Textile dyeing is one of the largest sources of water pollution, with toxic chemicals being discharged into rivers and oceans. These chemicals harm aquatic life and can contaminate drinking water sources, posing health risks to communities. Additionally, the energy required for fabric finishing and garment manufacturing predominantly comes from fossil fuels, further contributing to carbon emissions.

The environmental impact extends to the end of a garment's life cycle. The fast fashion model encourages a culture of disposability, where clothes are worn a few times and then discarded. This results in vast amounts of textile waste, much of which ends up in landfills. Synthetic fabrics, in particular, do not biodegrade and can persist in the environment for centuries. Even when clothing is incinerated, it releases harmful pollutants into the air. The linear model of take-make-dispose is clearly unsustainable and calls for a circular approach to fashion.

Embracing circular fashion involves designing for longevity, reusing, recycling, and regenerating materials. By prioritizing durable and timeless designs, we can reduce the need for frequent replacements. The practice of upcycling transforms old garments into new creations, adding value and reducing waste. Recycling initiatives can recover fibers from discarded clothes, turning them into new textiles. Additionally, biodegradable materials and closed-loop systems, where resources are continuously cycled, offer promising solutions. The shift towards circular fashion represents a holistic approach to sustainability, minimizing environmental impact at every stage of a garment's life.

4

Chapter 4: Ethical Fashion and Fair Trade

Ethical fashion goes beyond environmental considerations to encompass the social and economic dimensions of sustainability. It addresses the rights and well-being of the workers who make our clothes, ensuring fair wages, safe working conditions, and respect for labor rights. The fashion industry, particularly in developing countries, has been marred by exploitative practices, including low wages, long working hours, and unsafe factories. High-profile disasters like the Rana Plaza collapse in 2013 have highlighted the urgent need for reform and accountability.

Fair trade practices are central to ethical fashion, promoting equity and justice in the supply chain. Fair trade certification ensures that workers receive fair compensation for their labor and work in safe conditions. It also supports community development by investing in education, healthcare, and infrastructure. By choosing fair trade products, consumers can contribute to a more equitable global economy and empower the artisans and workers who create their clothes.

Transparency and traceability are key elements of ethical fashion. Brands committed to ethical practices disclose information about their supply chains, allowing consumers to make informed choices. This transparency builds trust and encourages accountability, as brands are held responsible for the conditions under which their products are made. Technology plays a crucial role in enhancing traceability, with innovations like blockchain providing secure and verifiable records of each step in the supply chain.

Consumer advocacy and activism are driving forces in the ethical fashion movement. Conscious consumers are demanding that brands uphold ethical standards and are using their purchasing power to support responsible businesses. Campaigns and initiatives like Fashion Revolution's #WhoMadeMyClothes encourage consumers to ask questions and seek transparency. By raising awareness and fostering a culture of accountability, we can create a fashion industry that respects the dignity and rights of all its workers.

5

Chapter 5: Innovations in Sustainable Materials

The quest for sustainable fashion has sparked a wave of innovation in materials science. Traditional textiles are being reimagined, and entirely new materials are emerging, offering more eco-friendly alternatives to conventional fabrics. This chapter delves into some of the most promising developments in sustainable materials, highlighting their potential to revolutionize the fashion industry.

One of the most exciting innovations is the development of bio-based materials, derived from renewable resources like plants and microorganisms. For example, Piñatex is a leather-like material made from pineapple leaf fibers, a byproduct of the pineapple industry. It's biodegradable and offers a sustainable alternative to animal leather. Similarly, mushroom leather, known as Mylo, is made from the root structure of mushrooms called mycelium. It's durable, flexible, and has a lower environmental footprint compared to traditional leather.

Recycling and upcycling initiatives are also gaining traction in the fashion world. Brands are increasingly using recycled materials, such as polyester made from post-consumer plastic bottles, to create new garments. Upcycling, the process of transforming waste materials into new products, is another creative solution. Designers are repurposing discarded textiles, vintage clothing, and industrial waste to craft unique and sustainable fashion pieces. These practices not only reduce waste but also add value and a unique story to each item.

Another promising area of innovation is the use of regenerative agriculture in textile production. Regenerative agriculture focuses on restoring and enhancing the health of ecosystems through practices like crop rotation, cover cropping, and reduced tillage. By growing fibers like cotton and hemp using regenerative methods, farmers can improve soil health, increase biodiversity, and sequester carbon. This approach not only yields sustainable raw materials but also contributes to the overall resilience of agricultural landscapes.

The future of sustainable materials lies in the hands of researchers, designers, and consumers who are willing to embrace new possibilities. By supporting and investing in these innovations, we can pave the way for a fashion industry that respects and nurtures the planet.

6

Chapter 6: The Role of Technology in Sustainable Fashion

Technology is playing a transformative role in advancing sustainable fashion. From smart textiles to digital design tools, technological innovations are enabling more efficient, transparent, and eco-friendly practices across the fashion industry. This chapter explores the intersection of technology and sustainability, showcasing how cutting-edge solutions are driving positive change.

One area where technology is making a significant impact is in the development of smart textiles. These are fabrics embedded with electronic components that can monitor and respond to environmental changes. For instance, thermoregulatory textiles can adjust their properties based on the wearer's body temperature, providing comfort while reducing the need for multiple layers of clothing. This can lead to a reduction in clothing consumption and waste. Additionally, some smart textiles are designed to biodegrade or break down into non-toxic components at the end of their life cycle, minimizing their environmental impact.

Digital design tools are revolutionizing the way fashion is created and produced. 3D modeling and virtual prototyping allow designers to visualize and test their ideas without the need for physical samples, reducing material waste and speeding up the design process. These tools also enable more precise and efficient pattern making, resulting in less fabric waste during production. Furthermore, digital platforms facilitate collaboration and transparency, allowing designers, manufacturers, and consumers to track the entire lifecycle of a garment.

Blockchain technology is another powerful tool for enhancing transparency and traceability in the fashion supply chain. By providing a secure and immutable record of each transaction, blockchain ensures that information about a garment's origin, materials, and production processes is accessible and verifiable. This transparency builds trust between brands and consumers and encourages ethical practices throughout the supply chain. It also empowers consumers to make informed choices and hold brands accountable for their environmental and social impact.

As technology continues to evolve, it holds the potential to drive even greater sustainability in fashion. By embracing these innovations and integrating them into their practices, brands can create a more responsible and resilient fashion industry. The future of fashion is not just about what we wear, but how we create it and the impact it has on the world.

7

Chapter 7: The Role of Fashion Designers in Sustainability

Fashion designers hold immense power in shaping the future of sustainable fashion. They are the visionaries who bring ideas to life, setting trends and influencing consumer behavior. This chapter explores how designers can lead the charge towards sustainability by embracing eco-friendly practices, innovative materials, and ethical considerations.

Designers have the unique ability to integrate sustainability into their creative process from the very beginning. By prioritizing environmentally friendly materials and reducing waste, they can create collections that are both stylish and sustainable. For example, zero-waste design techniques involve carefully planning patterns to minimize fabric scraps. This approach not only conserves resources but also challenges designers to think creatively and push the boundaries of traditional design.

Collaboration is key to advancing sustainability in fashion. Designers can work with scientists, engineers, and manufacturers to develop and implement innovative solutions. For instance, partnerships with material scientists can lead to the creation of new, sustainable textiles. Collaboration with production facilities can ensure that garments are made using ethical and eco-friendly methods. By fostering a culture of collaboration, designers can drive systemic change in the fashion industry.

Education and advocacy are also crucial components of a designer's role in sustainability. By raising awareness and educating consumers about the impact of their choices, designers can inspire more conscious consumption. This can be achieved through transparent communication about the materials and processes used in their collections, as well as promoting the benefits of sustainable fashion. Additionally, designers can use their platforms to advocate for policies and practices that support sustainability, such as regulations on waste and emissions, or incentives for sustainable innovation.

Ultimately, the future of sustainable fashion lies in the hands of designers who are willing to challenge the status quo and envision a new paradigm. By embracing their role as change-makers, designers can create a fashion industry that respects the planet and its people.

8

Chapter 8: Consumer Empowerment and Conscious Consumption

Consumers play a pivotal role in the shift towards sustainable fashion. Their choices and behaviors drive demand, influencing the practices of brands and retailers. This chapter delves into the concept of conscious consumption, exploring how consumers can make informed and responsible decisions that support sustainability.

Conscious consumption begins with awareness. By educating themselves about the environmental and social impact of their clothing choices, consumers can make more informed decisions. This involves understanding the materials and processes used in garment production, as well as the ethical practices of the brands they support. Transparency and traceability are essential tools in this process, allowing consumers to verify the claims made by brands and ensure that their purchases align with their values.

The power of choice extends beyond individual purchases. By supporting brands that prioritize sustainability, consumers can drive positive change in the fashion industry. This can involve choosing products made from organic or recycled materials, buying from ethical and fair-trade brands, or supporting local and independent designers. By voting with their wallets, consumers can send a strong message to the industry that sustainability matters.

Reducing consumption is another key aspect of conscious fashion. The fast fashion model encourages a culture of overconsumption, where garments are worn a few times and then discarded. To counter this, consumers can adopt practices such as buying less but better, prioritizing quality over quantity, and investing in timeless, versatile pieces that can be worn for years. Additionally, embracing second-hand and vintage shopping, as well as clothing swaps and rentals, can extend the life of garments and reduce waste.

Repairing and maintaining clothing is another powerful way for consumers to contribute to sustainability. Simple practices like mending tears, sewing on buttons, and properly caring for garments can significantly extend their lifespan. By valuing and taking care of their clothes, consumers can reduce the demand for new products and minimize their environmental footprint.

Conscious consumption is about more than just making responsible choices; it's about fostering a deeper connection with the items we wear and the impact they have on the world. By embracing this mindset, consumers can be active participants in the movement towards a more sustainable and ethical fashion industry.

9

Chapter 9: The Intersection of Fashion and Climate Change

Fashion is intrinsically linked to climate change, both as a contributor to the problem and a potential part of the solution. The industry is responsible for a significant portion of global greenhouse gas emissions, from the production of raw materials to the transportation of finished products. This chapter explores the ways in which fashion impacts the climate and how it can play a role in mitigating climate change.

The production of textiles, particularly synthetic fibers like polyester, is energy-intensive and heavily reliant on fossil fuels. This results in substantial carbon emissions throughout the manufacturing process. Additionally, the cultivation of natural fibers such as cotton often involves the use of water-intensive irrigation methods and chemical inputs, further exacerbating environmental degradation. The cumulative impact of these practices contributes to global warming and environmental instability.

Transportation is another major source of emissions within the fashion industry. Garments are often produced in regions with low labor costs and then shipped around the world to reach consumers. This extensive supply chain results in significant carbon emissions from shipping and air freight. By shortening supply chains, localizing production, and adopting more efficient transportation methods, the industry can reduce its carbon footprint.

Innovative solutions are emerging to address fashion's climate impact. Carbon offset programs allow brands to invest in projects that reduce or capture carbon emissions, such as reforestation and renewable energy initiatives. Furthermore, adopting sustainable practices like using renewable energy in manufacturing, improving energy efficiency, and prioritizing low-impact materials can significantly reduce the industry's carbon footprint. The integration of circular economy principles, such as recycling and upcycling, also contributes to climate mitigation by minimizing waste and resource consumption.

Consumer behavior plays a crucial role in shaping the industry's response to climate change. By choosing sustainable and ethically produced garments, supporting brands with robust environmental policies, and advocating for systemic change, consumers can drive demand for climate-conscious fashion. The collective efforts of consumers, brands, and policymakers can pave the way for a fashion industry that aligns with global climate goals and fosters a sustainable future.

10

Chapter 10: The Cultural Significance of Sustainable Fashion

Fashion is not just about clothing; it is a powerful cultural force that reflects and shapes societal values, identities, and movements. The rise of sustainable fashion is intertwined with a broader cultural shift towards environmental consciousness and social responsibility. This chapter delves into the cultural significance of sustainable fashion, exploring how it influences and is influenced by contemporary society.

Sustainable fashion represents a return to values that prioritize quality, longevity, and craftsmanship. In contrast to the disposable culture of fast fashion, sustainable fashion encourages consumers to cherish and care for their garments. This shift is reflected in the resurgence of traditional crafts and artisanal techniques, where clothing is imbued with meaning and heritage. By valuing the stories behind the garments, consumers can develop a deeper connection to their wardrobe and the people who create it.

The movement towards sustainable fashion is also closely linked to the broader environmental and social justice movements. It challenges the exploitative practices that have long plagued the fashion industry, advocating for fair wages, safe working conditions, and respect for workers' rights. This alignment with social justice resonates with a new generation of consumers who seek to make a positive impact through their choices. Fashion becomes a medium for expressing values, activism, and solidarity with global communities.

Cultural icons and influencers play a significant role in promoting sustainable fashion. Celebrities, designers, and activists who champion eco-friendly practices can raise awareness and inspire change on a large scale. Their endorsements bring sustainable fashion into the mainstream, making it accessible and desirable to a wider audience. By using their platforms to advocate for sustainability, these cultural figures amplify the message and encourage collective action.

Sustainable fashion also intersects with local and indigenous cultures, celebrating diversity and preserving heritage. Traditional textiles, techniques, and designs offer valuable insights into sustainable practices that have stood the test of time. By honoring and integrating these cultural elements, the fashion industry can foster a more inclusive and respectful approach to sustainability. The cultural richness of sustainable fashion lies in its ability to bridge the past and present, creating a future that respects and cherishes both people and the planet.

11

Chapter 11: Circular Economy and Fashion

The concept of a circular economy offers a transformative approach to sustainability in the fashion industry. Unlike the traditional linear model of take-make-dispose, a circular economy aims to keep resources in use for as long as possible, extracting maximum value before recovering and regenerating products and materials. This chapter explores how the principles of a circular economy can be applied to fashion, creating a system that is restorative and regenerative by design.

At the heart of a circular fashion economy is the idea of designing out waste and pollution. This involves creating garments that are durable, repairable, and recyclable. Designers play a crucial role in this process, considering the entire lifecycle of a product from the outset. By choosing sustainable materials, designing for modularity, and incorporating easy-to-repair elements, they can ensure that garments have a long and useful life. Additionally, implementing take-back schemes and recycling programs allows brands to recover materials and reintegrate them into the production process.

Upcycling and repurposing are key strategies in a circular fashion economy. Upcycling involves transforming waste materials or old garments into new products of higher value. This creative approach not only reduces waste but also adds a unique touch to each piece, making it stand out in the market.

Repurposing, on the other hand, involves finding new uses for existing products or materials, extending their lifespan and reducing the need for new resources. These practices challenge the traditional notions of fashion and encourage a more sustainable mindset.

Digital technologies also play a significant role in enabling a circular fashion economy. Tools like 3D printing, digital pattern making, and virtual sampling allow for precise and efficient production, minimizing waste and resource use. Blockchain technology enhances transparency and traceability, ensuring that materials and products can be tracked throughout their lifecycle. This enables better recycling and waste management practices, as well as fostering trust between brands and consumers.

The transition to a circular fashion economy requires collaboration and innovation across the entire supply chain. Brands, designers, manufacturers, and consumers all have a part to play in creating a system that values sustainability and resilience. By embracing circularity, the fashion industry can reduce its environmental impact, create economic opportunities, and contribute to a more sustainable future.

12

Chapter 12: The Power of Policy and Regulation

Government policies and regulations play a crucial role in shaping the sustainability landscape of the fashion industry. Effective policies can drive positive change, incentivize sustainable practices, and hold brands accountable for their environmental and social impact. This chapter explores the role of policy and regulation in promoting sustainable fashion and the key measures that can support the transition.

One of the most impactful policies is the implementation of extended producer responsibility (EPR) schemes. EPR places the responsibility for the entire lifecycle of a product, including its disposal, on the producer. In the context of fashion, this means that brands would be accountable for the end-of-life management of their garments, incentivizing them to design for durability, repairability, and recyclability. EPR schemes can reduce waste, promote recycling, and encourage more sustainable production practices.

Another important regulatory measure is the establishment of environmental standards and certifications. These standards set benchmarks for sustainable practices, such as the use of organic materials, reduction of water and energy consumption, and minimization of chemical use. Certifications like the Global Organic Textile Standard (GOTS) and OEKO-TEX provide assurance to consumers that the products they purchase meet these standards. By promoting and enforcing environmental standards, governments can ensure that the fashion industry operates in a more sustainable and responsible manner.

Transparency and traceability are also critical components of effective policy. Regulations that require brands to disclose information about their supply chains, materials, and production processes can enhance accountability and empower consumers to make informed choices. Policies that mandate transparent labeling and reporting can help build trust and drive demand for sustainable products. Additionally, the use of digital technologies like blockchain can support traceability efforts, providing secure and verifiable records of a garment's journey from raw material to finished product.

Collaboration between governments, industry stakeholders, and civil society is essential for the success of sustainable fashion policies. Multi-stakeholder initiatives, such as the Fashion Pact and the Sustainable Apparel Coalition, bring together brands, policymakers, and NGOs to develop and implement solutions for a more sustainable industry. By working together, these entities can create a cohesive framework that supports sustainability and drives meaningful change.

The power of policy and regulation lies in its ability to set the agenda and create the conditions for a sustainable fashion industry. By implementing and enforcing robust policies, governments can steer the industry towards practices that respect the environment and uphold social justice, contributing to a more sustainable and equitable future.

13

Chapter 13: Community-Based Fashion Initiatives

Community-based fashion initiatives offer a powerful model for sustainable and ethical fashion. These initiatives are rooted in local communities, leveraging traditional knowledge, skills, and resources to create garments that are both sustainable and socially empowering. This chapter explores how community-based fashion initiatives can drive positive change and foster a sense of connection and resilience.

At the heart of community-based fashion is the emphasis on local production and supply chains. By sourcing materials locally and employing artisans from the community, these initiatives reduce the environmental impact associated with long-distance transportation and support the local economy. This approach also helps preserve traditional crafts and techniques, ensuring that valuable cultural heritage is passed down through generations. Examples of such initiatives include cooperatives of weavers and dyers in India, indigenous textile projects in Latin America, and artisanal fashion collectives in Africa.

Empowerment and social equity are central to community-based fashion initiatives. By providing fair wages, safe working conditions, and opportunities for skill development, these initiatives uplift artisans and workers, giving them a sense of ownership and pride in their work. This empowerment extends beyond economic benefits; it fosters a sense of community and collaboration, creating a supportive network that strengthens social bonds. Initiatives like the Fair Trade movement and the Global Mamas project in Ghana exemplify how community-based fashion can lead to transformative social change.

Sustainability is inherently woven into the fabric of community-based fashion. The emphasis on locally sourced, natural, and renewable materials minimizes environmental impact. Additionally, the focus on quality and craftsmanship ensures that garments are durable and cherished, reducing the need for frequent replacements. By adopting practices like natural dyeing, hand weaving, and zero-waste pattern making, these initiatives demonstrate that traditional methods can be both eco-friendly and innovative.

The success of community-based fashion initiatives relies on the support and participation of consumers. By choosing to purchase from these initiatives, consumers can contribute to the preservation of cultural heritage, the empowerment of artisans, and the promotion of sustainable practices. This conscious choice creates a positive feedback loop, where demand for ethical and sustainable fashion drives further investment in community-based projects. Through collective action and collaboration, we can build a fashion industry that values people, planet, and tradition.

14

Chapter 14: The Future of Fashion: Trends and Predictions

The future of fashion is being shaped by a confluence of sustainability, technology, and cultural shifts. As the industry continues to evolve, new trends and innovations are emerging that promise to redefine the way we create, consume, and experience fashion. This chapter explores some of the key trends and predictions for the future of sustainable fashion.

One of the most significant trends is the rise of circular fashion, where garments are designed for longevity, repairability, and recyclability. This shift towards a circular economy is driven by increasing awareness of the environmental impact of fast fashion and the need for more sustainable practices. Brands are embracing circular design principles, creating products that can be easily disassembled and recycled at the end of their life cycle. This approach not only reduces waste but also conserves valuable resources and fosters a culture of sustainability.

Technology is playing a transformative role in the future of fashion. Advances in digital tools, such as 3D printing, virtual prototyping, and augmented reality, are revolutionizing the design and production process. These technologies enable more efficient use of materials, reduce waste, and allow for greater customization and personalization. For example, consumers can use augmented reality to virtually try on clothes, reducing the need for physical samples and returns. Additionally, blockchain technology is enhancing transparency and traceability, ensuring that garments are ethically and sustainably produced.

The concept of "slow fashion" is gaining momentum as consumers seek to build more meaningful connections with their clothing. Slow fashion emphasizes quality over quantity, encouraging consumers to invest in timeless, well-made pieces that can be worn and cherished for years. This trend is supported by the resurgence of traditional crafts and artisanal techniques, as well as the growing popularity of second-hand and vintage fashion. By valuing the stories behind the garments and the people who create them, slow fashion fosters a deeper appreciation for clothing and its impact on the world.

Sustainability is becoming a core value for fashion brands and consumers alike. As awareness of environmental and social issues grows, brands are increasingly adopting sustainable practices and transparent supply chains. Consumers are demanding greater accountability and are willing to support brands that align with their values. This shift is driving innovation and encouraging the fashion industry to rethink its approach to design, production, and consumption. The future of fashion is one where sustainability is not just an option but a fundamental principle guiding every decision.

15

Chapter 15: Educational Initiatives and Sustainable Fashion

Education is a cornerstone of the sustainable fashion movement. By raising awareness and providing knowledge, educational initiatives can empower individuals and communities to make informed and responsible choices. This chapter explores the role of education in promoting sustainable fashion and the various ways in which knowledge can be disseminated and shared.

Fashion schools and universities play a pivotal role in shaping the future of the industry. By incorporating sustainability into their curricula, these institutions can equip the next generation of designers, merchandisers, and business leaders with the skills and mindset needed to drive positive change. Courses on sustainable materials, ethical production practices, and circular economy principles provide students with a comprehensive understanding of the complexities of the fashion industry. Additionally, hands-on projects and collaborations with sustainable brands offer valuable real-world experience and inspire innovative solutions.

Public awareness campaigns are another powerful tool for educating consumers about sustainable fashion. These campaigns can take many forms, from social media initiatives and documentary films to workshops and community events. By highlighting the environmental and social impact of fashion, these campaigns encourage individuals to reflect on their consumption habits and consider more sustainable alternatives. Initiatives like Fashion Revolution's #WhoMadeMyClothes campaign have successfully raised awareness and sparked conversations about transparency and ethics in the fashion industry.

Educational resources, such as books, blogs, podcasts, and online courses, provide accessible and engaging ways for people to learn about sustainable fashion. These resources offer insights into the latest trends, technologies, and best practices, making sustainability knowledge more widely available. By sharing stories of successful sustainable fashion projects and showcasing innovative solutions, these resources inspire and empower individuals to take action in their own lives.

Collaborative learning and peer-to-peer education also play a significant role in promoting sustainable fashion. Community groups, online forums, and social media platforms offer spaces for individuals to share knowledge, experiences, and tips on sustainable living. These platforms foster a sense of community and collective action, where people can learn from one another and support each other's sustainability journeys. By building networks of like-minded individuals, we can amplify the impact of sustainable fashion education and create a culture of shared responsibility.

Ultimately, education is the foundation upon which a sustainable fashion industry can be built. By raising awareness, providing knowledge, and fostering a culture of continuous learning, we can empower individuals and communities to make choices that support a sustainable and ethical future.

16

Chapter 16: The Intersection of Art and Sustainable Fashion

Fashion is a form of art that reflects creativity, individuality, and cultural expression. The intersection of art and sustainable fashion offers a unique and powerful platform for advocating sustainability and inspiring change. This chapter explores how artists and designers are using their creative talents to promote sustainable fashion and the impact of their work on the industry and society.

Artistic expression in fashion can take many forms, from innovative designs and upcycled creations to immersive installations and performances. By pushing the boundaries of traditional fashion, artists challenge our perceptions and encourage us to think differently about clothing and consumption. Their work often highlights the beauty and potential of sustainable materials, demonstrating that eco-friendly fashion can be both innovative and aesthetically pleasing.

Collaborations between artists and sustainable fashion brands are becoming increasingly common. These partnerships bring together the creativity of the artist and the resources of the brand to create unique and impactful projects. For example, designers may work with artists to develop limited-edition collections made from upcycled or recycled materials. These collaborations not only result in distinctive and desirable products but also raise awareness about sustainability and support the brand's commitment to ethical practices.

Artistic activism is a powerful tool for advocating for sustainable fashion. Artists use their work to draw attention to environmental and social issues, provoke thought, and inspire action. This can take the form of visual art, such as paintings and sculptures that depict the impact of fashion on the environment, or performance art that explores themes of consumption and waste. By engaging audiences on an emotional and intellectual level, artistic activism can drive meaningful change and foster a deeper understanding of the need for sustainable practices.

Fashion shows and exhibitions are another platform for showcasing sustainable fashion as an art form. These events provide an opportunity for designers and artists to present their work to a wider audience, celebrate creativity, and promote sustainability. They also offer a space for dialogue and collaboration, where industry professionals, consumers, and activists can come together to share ideas and explore new possibilities. By elevating sustainable fashion within the realm of art, these events help to legitimize and mainstream eco-friendly practices.

The intersection of art and sustainable fashion is a testament to the power of creativity and innovation in driving change. By harnessing the artistic talents of designers and artists, we can create a fashion industry that not only values sustainability but also celebrates beauty, individuality, and cultural expression.

Book Description:

In "Threads of the Earth: How Fashion, Ecology, and Ethics Weave a Sustainable Future," embark on a captivating journey that unravels the complex relationship between the fashion industry, the environment, and our collective responsibility. This book delves into the intricate fabric of our lives, revealing how our choices in clothing affect the planet and the people who inhabit it.

Each chapter of this thought-provoking book explores a different facet of sustainable fashion, from the ancient wisdom of indigenous textile practices to cutting-edge innovations in bio-based materials. Discover how designers

CHAPTER 16: THE INTERSECTION OF ART AND SUSTAINABLE FASHION

are leading the charge towards eco-friendly fashion, and how consumers can make conscious choices that support a more sustainable future.

Through vivid storytelling and detailed analysis, "Threads of the Earth" sheds light on the environmental impact of fashion, the power of ethical and fair trade practices, and the potential of a circular economy. It highlights the role of technology in driving positive change, the significance of educational initiatives, and the cultural richness of sustainable fashion.

This book is a call to action for designers, consumers, policymakers, and industry leaders to come together and create a fashion industry that values people, planet, and tradition. With practical insights, inspiring stories, and a vision for the future, "Threads of the Earth" offers a roadmap for weaving a more sustainable and ethical world through fashion.

www.ingramcontent.com/pod-product-compliance
Lightning Source LLC
LaVergne TN
LVHW020739090526
838202LV00057BA/6088